CATS SET VII

SINGAPURA CATS

Kristin Petrie
ABDO Publishing Company

visit us at
www.abdopublishing.com

Printed in the United States of America, North Mankato, Minnesota.
052013
092013

PRINTED ON RECYCLED PAPER

Cover Photo: Photo by Helmi Flick
Interior Photos: Alamy pp. 9, 15, 17, 20–21; AP Images p. 19; Corbis p. 21;
    Glow Images pp. 5, 7, 13; Photo by Helmi Flick p. 11

Editors: Rochelle Baltzer, Megan M. Gunderson
Art Direction: Neil Klinepier

Library of Congress Control Number: 2013932674

Cataloging-in-Publication Data

Petrie, Kristin.
 Singapura cats / Kristin Petrie.
   p. cm. -- (Cats)
ISBN 978-1-61783-867-5
Includes bibliographical references and index.
1. Singapura cat--Juvenile literature.   I. Title.
636.8--dc23

2013932674

CONTENTS

LIONS, TIGERS, AND CATS

Cats! They come in many sizes, shapes, and colors. The mighty lion is a member of the cat family. The hairless sphynx is also a member! Whether big, small, hairy, or hairless, all cats are from the family **Felidae**.

The family Felidae is 37 members strong. Originally, this family consisted of only wild cats. Then around 3,500 years ago, humans began **domesticating** the wild creatures.

Some humans appreciated the cat's hunting abilities. These skilled mousers kept pests away from stored food. Other people recognized the cat as a friendly companion.

Over time, humans **bred** different **domestic** cats to have certain desirable qualities. Today, there are more than 40 breeds! If you want a cat that loves to be around people, the Singapura is a perfect choice.

SINGAPURA CATS

    Singapura is the Malaysian word for Singapore. Knowing this, one can easily guess where the Singapura cat is from. Singapore!

    There, the cats were simply known as street, sewer, or drain cats. The **breed**'s exact origin is unknown. However, its coat color and pattern are both found in cats from Southeast Asia.

    Americans Hal and Tommy Meadow brought the first Singapura cats to the United States in the early 1970s. There, breeders worked to maintain the Singapura's playful character. They also preserved its desire to be around people.

    The **Cat Fanciers' Association** first accepted the breed for registration in 1982. Today,

Singapura cats are found around the world. They remain rare, but those who know the **breed** love the breed!

In 1991, the government of Singapore recognized the Singapura as a national treasure.

QUALITIES

The Singapura is a highly affectionate **breed**. Your Singapura will want to be with you or on you at all times! This makes the breed dearly loved by many, but too needy for others.

Singapuras love and seek constant attention. They are best suited for families that are home a lot. For busy families, having other cats can help provide interaction. Singapuras also get along well with children, but they don't like loud noises.

The Singapura is a curious, intelligent cat. It wants to be involved in human activities, whether it's invited or not. It will play with a pen or keyboard you're trying to use. And, it will crawl in bed with you. Some even say a Singapura can tell when its owner is feeling down.

Some cats are described as wanting "four on the floor," but that is not the Singapura. It will leap onto high cabinets or the refrigerator just to keep an eye on everything. Or, it will hop up on your shoulders to stay a part of the action!

A Singapura's voice is quiet, but it may meow a lot!

COAT AND COLOR

The Singapura's coat color is called sepia agouti. This special color is an old ivory base color with a dark brown **ticked tabby** pattern. In this pattern, individual hairs have bands of light and dark color. All strands end in a dark tip.

The Singapura's chest, **muzzle**, and chin are lighter in color. The inside of each front leg has signature markings, or barring. These markings are also on the knee of each rear leg.

Unlike many **breeds**, the Singapura has only one layer of hair. There is no downy undercoat. The single layer is short and silky. It lies close to the skin, giving the breed its sleek look.

Like many **breeds** that require little grooming, the Singapura is called a "wash and wear" cat. Brushing twice a month will maintain the healthy, shiny coat. Simply choose a comb or brush designed for the Singapura's short coat.

The Singapura's tail is slightly shorter than its body. The tip of the tail is dark. This color extends along the top of the tail back to the body.

SIZE

The sleek Singapura is the smallest **pedigreed** cat **breed**. Females are dainty, weighing just four to five pounds (1.8 to 2.3 kg). Males are slightly larger, weighing up to eight pounds (3.2 kg).

Do not let the Singapura's small size fool you! These cats look lighter than they feel because their bodies are muscular. These little powerhouses stand on long, strong legs that end in small paws.

The Singapura's large, almond-shaped eyes are its most notable feature. They come in a range of captivating colors, including green, hazel, yellow, gold, and copper.

The Singapura also has very large ears. Angled slightly back, the ears give a highly alert appearance. A signature M-shaped marking rests between the ears. Other black markings extend from the corners of the eyes to the nose.

Don't choose a kitten based on eye color. The color may change as the kitten grows up!

CARE

Like all pets, the Singapura requires good care. At home, cats need regular teeth brushing. Toothpaste and toothbrushes made specially for cats are readily available. Brushing your cat's teeth removes bacteria and tartar. This keeps the teeth clean and your pet healthy.

About every two weeks, trim your cat's claws. This will prevent scratching of people and furniture. Cats appreciate a scratching post for naturally filing their claws, too. Plus, the energetic Singapura will love to climb it!

Singapuras do not have special health concerns. However, due to their small size, females may have difficulty giving birth. If trouble arises, a veterinarian can perform surgery to deliver kittens.

Singapuras also need yearly visits to the veterinarian. He or she will provide **vaccines** and do a wellness exam. The veterinarian will also **spay** or **neuter** kittens that will not be **bred**.

Singapuras are sometimes called "Puras" for short.

FEEDING

The Singapura requires a balanced diet and plenty of water. Carbohydrates supply energy. Proteins keep their muscular bodies strong. Fats nourish skin, coat, and more. Vitamins and minerals build bones and prevent illness.

Thankfully, quality balanced cat foods are easy to find. They come in different varieties including moist, semimoist, and dry. Moist food can spoil, so don't leave it out too long. Dry food stays fresh the longest. And, it helps clean your cat's teeth.

Singapuras are active cats. You must feed them enough, but not too much! If a Singapura gets too much food, it will lose its sleek shape. A cat without enough food has a visible rib cage and feels bony. Be sure your cat gets the right balance.

Clean, fresh water should always be available for your Singapura.

KITTENS

Singapura cats are slower to mature than most **breeds**. They are not ready to reproduce until they are at least one year old.

After mating, a mother Singapura is **pregnant** for about 65 days. Then, she delivers a **litter** of just two to three kittens. Singapura kittens are very tiny as well as helpless. Their mother cares for them completely until they can see and hear. That is 10 to 12 dark days after birth.

Kittens **wean** naturally when their teeth start to appear. This is at about 5 weeks of age. However, they continue to nurse for several more weeks. Then, kittens eat just solid food. Special varieties are available to give their growing bodies just what they need.

Singapura kittens don't reach full size until 15 to 24 months.

Between 12 and 16 weeks, Singapura kittens are ready to leave their mother. At this time, they are healthy and strong. They have received their first **vaccines** and they are **socialized**.

BUYING A KITTEN

Is a Singapura cat right for you? This question must be considered carefully. Singapuras are affectionate and very interactive. They require activity and company from their owners. People wanting a low-maintenance, independent cat should look for a different **breed**!

If a Singapura is your dream cat, locate a reputable breeder. Singapuras remain somewhat rare, so you may be put on a waiting list for a kitten. Sometimes, adopting an

The Singapura's curious, playful nature isn't just for kittens. It lasts into old age.

adult Singapura is a faster option. A loving cat in need of a home may be available from a **breed** rescue.

Singapuras may bond with one family member or all of them. And, they are not usually afraid of strangers.

If a kitten is your wish, be patient and look for a healthy one. A healthy kitten has a shiny coat, clear eyes and ears, and a cool, moist nose. Many breeders provide a written health guarantee for their kittens. Once home, enjoy your lively and lovable Singapura! He or she will be with you for 9 to 15 years.

Glossary

breed - a group of animals sharing the same ancestors and appearance. A breeder is a person who raises animals. Raising animals is often called breeding them.

Cat Fanciers' Association - a group that sets the standards for judging all breeds of cats.

domestic - tame, especially relating to animals. To domesticate is to adapt something to life with humans.

Felidae (FEHL-uh-dee) - the scientific Latin name for the cat family. Members of this family are called felids. They include lions, tigers, leopards, jaguars, cougars, wildcats, lynx, cheetahs, and domestic cats.

litter - all of the kittens born at one time to a mother cat.

muzzle - an animal's nose and jaws.

neuter (NOO-tuhr) - to remove a male animal's reproductive glands.

pedigreed - relating to having a record of an animal's ancestors.

pregnant - having one or more babies growing within the body.

socialize - to adapt an animal to behaving properly around people or other animals in various settings.

spay - to remove a female animal's reproductive organs.

tabby - a coat pattern featuring stripes or splotches of a dark color on a lighter background. Individual hairs are banded with light and dark colors.

ticked - having hair banded with two or more colors.

vaccine (vak-SEEN) - a shot given to prevent illness or disease.

wean - to accustom an animal to eating food other than its mother's milk.

WEB SITES

To learn more about Singapura cats, visit ABDO Publishing Company online. Web sites about Singapura cats are featured on our Book Links page. These links are routinely monitored and updated to provide the most current information available.

www.abdopublishing.com

INDEX